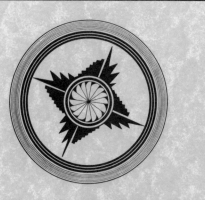

"PELICANS"

by Lynn M. Stone

Rourke Enterprises, Inc.
Vero Beach, Florida 32964

Library of Congress Cataloging-in-Publication Data

Stone, Lynn M.
  Pelicans

  (The Bird discovery library)
  Includes index.
  Summary: Examines the pelican, describing its habitat, physical
characteristics, behavior, and relationship with people, with an
emphasis on the brown and white pelicans.
  1. Brown pelican—Juvenile literature. 2. White pelican—
Juvenile literature. [1. Brown pelican. 2. White pelican. 3.
Pelicans] I. Title.
II. Series: Stone, Lynn M. Bird discovery library.
QL696.P47S76 1989   598.4'3   88-26428
ISBN 0-86592-322-1

TABLE OF CONTENTS

PELICANS

Pelicans are large, fish-eating birds that live near water. The Pelican is easy to identify—it has a king-sized throat pouch. "A wonderful bird is the pelican," wrote poet Dixon Lanier Merritt, "His bill will hold more than his belican."

Two of the world's seven **species,** or kinds, of pelicans live in North America. They are the brown pelican *(Pelecanus occidentalis)* and the white pelican *(Pelecanus erythrorhyncos).*

Pelicans live to be quite old. Captive pelicans have lived more than 25 years.

Great White Pelican
(Pelecanus onocrotalus)
of Europe, Asia, and Africa

WHERE THEY LIVE

Pelicans live in many countries. They live where the air and water are fairly warm, where they can catch fish, and where they can safely nest.

Each species has its own special needs. For example, the brown pelican lives all year along the sea coasts of South America and southern North America. The white pelican spends the warm months inland on big, shallow lakes in western North America. In the autumn, white pelicans **migrate,** or travel, south to warmer places because their summer homes become too cold.

Brown Pelican with Full Pouch

HOW THEY LOOK

Pelicans have long necks and plump bodies. The famous pouch is attached to a foot-long beak and the pelican's neck. On land, pelicans waddle like ducks. They have stubby legs and flat, webbed feet.

Pelicans in flight are streamlined and fast. Their wings are long and narrow, up to nine feet across. They are ideal for gliding.

American white pelicans weigh up to 15 pounds and measure 50 inches from bill to tail. They are larger than brown pelicans.

Brown Pelican in Flight

THE PELICAN'S POUCH

People once thought that pelicans carried live fish in their pouches, as if the pouches were goldfish bowls. Pelicans use their pouches to catch fish, not to store or carry them.

The pelican's pouch is made of thin skin called **membrane.** The skin stretches when the pouch fills with water—up to three and one-half gallons of it!

On hot days pelicans use their pouches to help cool off. The surface area of the big pouch helps the pelican release body heat.

Brown Pelican with Full Pouch

Brown Pelican Taking Off
from Water

THE PELICAN'S DAY

Pelicans spend many daytime hours fishing. Afterwards they rest and preen.

When a pelican preens, it cleans and oils its feathers. The oil comes from tiny, hidden pouches called **glands.** A pelican applies oil to its feathers by using the tip of its bill. The oil helps keep the feathers waterproof, like a raincoat. Clean, oiled feathers keep the pelican from sinking when it is swimming.

At sunset, pelicans fly to islands where they rest until morning.

Brown Pelican, Young Adult, with Fish

PELICAN NESTS

When they begin to build nests, pelicans gather together in groups called **colonies.** Each nesting pelican lays two or three eggs in a nest built of grass and sticks. The nests are almost always on islands.

White pelicans nest on the ground or in floating nests made of marsh plants. Brown pelicans nest on the ground or in trees.

White pelicans grow a ''horn'' on their bill at nesting time. Brown pelicans don't grow ''horns,'' but their **plumage**—their covering of feathers—changes color at nesting time. The neck feathers change from white to yellow.

After nesting begins, the white pelican's horn fall off, and the brown pelican's plumage changes again.

Brown Pelican Baby in Down

BABY PELICANS

After a month of **incubation,** the time when the pelican sits on the eggs to keep them warm, pelican eggs hatch. The babies have no feathers, and they are helpless. But because they live on islands, few enemies ever reach them.

Baby pelicans squawk when they are hungry. They eat bits of fish which their parents cough up for them.

They are soon covered by **down**—soft, fluffy features. By the time they are 10 to 12 weeks old, they have lost their voices and the down has been replaced by heavier feathers. Now the young pelicans can fly from their nests.

American White Pelican
Feeding Baby

PREY

Pelicans feed on almost nothing except fish. Fish are the pelicans' **prey,** the animals which they hunt for food.

White pelicans swim in flocks and herd fish together. Then the pelicans can easily scoop the fish into their pouches.

The brown pelican usually hunts by flying over salt water. It has excellent eyesight and can spy fish swimming near the surface of the ocean. It dives for the fish, crashing headfirst into the sea. A pelican drains water from its pouch by tipping its head forward. Then it tosses its head upward to swallow the fish.

Brown Pelicans Diving for Fish

PELICANS AND PEOPLE

People enjoy watching pelicans, and our laws protect pelicans in North America. But people also cause problems for pelicans.

Sometimes people catch too many fish from one place. Then pelicans do not have enough to eat.

In some areas, people frighten pelicans from their nests. In places where both people and pelicans catch fish, pelicans often become caught in the hooks and line of fishermen.

Man-made poisons that spill into the water and poison fish also kill pelicans. Pelicans that eat the poisoned fish are themselves poisoned.

If we help protect their homes and their source of food, we will always be able to enjoy wild pelicans.

GLOSSARY

Colonies (KAHL uh neez)—a group of nesting animals of the same kind

Down (DOWN)—soft, tiny feathers

Gland (GLAND)—a small pouch which stores liquid, such as oil

Incubate (INK you bate)—to keep eggs wam until they hatch

Membrane (MEM brane)—soft, thin skin

Migrate (MY grate)—to move or fly one place to another at the same time each year

Plumage (PLOO maj)—the covering of feathers on a bird

Preen (PREEN)—to carefully clean and oil feathers

Prey (PRAY)—an animal which is hunted for food by another animal

Species (SPEE sheez)—within a group of closely-related animals, such as pelicans, one certain type

INDEX